GET A LIFE!

WILLIAM THE CONQUEROR

Books in the GET A LIFE! series

GET A LIFE!
WILLIAM THE CONQUEROR

PHILIP ARDAGH

Illustrated by Alan Rowe

MACMILLAN CHILDREN'S BOOKS

This one's for 'Harold',
Lord Kings Norton,
Baron of Wotton Underwood.
Miss you.

First published 1999
by Macmillan Children's Books
a division of Macmillan Publishers Ltd
25 Eccleston Place, London SW1W 9NF
Basingstoke and Oxford
www.macmillan.co.uk

Associated companies throughout the world

ISBN 0 330 37505 9

Text copyright © Philip Ardagh 1999
Illustrations copyright © Alan Rowe 1999

1 3 5 7 9 8 6 4 2

A CIP catalogue record for this book is available from the British Library.

Printed by Mackays of Chatham plc, Chatham, Kent.

CONTENTS

The Author's Ever-so-Accurate
FAMILY TREE OF
WILLIAM THE CONQUEROR
with people left out here and there to make things fit and look pretty

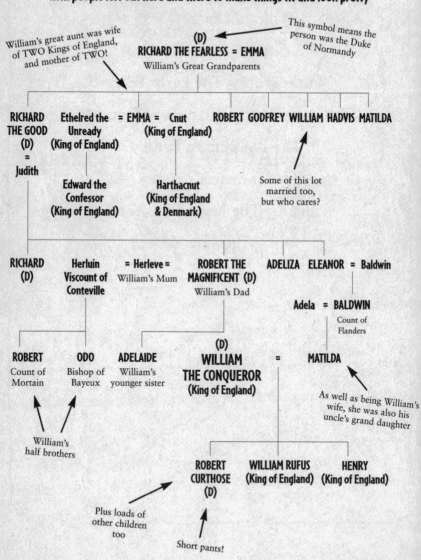

This symbol means the person was the Duke of Normandy

(D)
RICHARD THE FEARLESS = EMMA
William's Great Grandparents

William's great aunt was wife of TWO Kings of England, and mother of TWO!

RICHARD THE GOOD (D) = **Judith**

Ethelred the Unready (King of England) = **EMMA** = **Cnut (King of England)**

ROBERT GODFREY WILLIAM HADVIS MATILDA

Edward the Confessor (King of England)

Harthacnut (King of England & Denmark)

Some of this lot married too, but who cares?

RICHARD (D)

Herluin Viscount of Conteville = **Herleve** = William's Mum

ROBERT THE MAGNIFICENT (D) William's Dad

ADELIZA ELEANOR = Baldwin

Adela = BALDWIN Count of Flanders

ROBERT Count of Mortain

ODO Bishop of Bayeux

ADELAIDE William's younger sister

(D) WILLIAM THE CONQUEROR (King of England) = **MATILDA**

William's half brothers

As well as being William's wife, she was also his uncle's grand daughter

ROBERT CURTHOSE (D)

WILLIAM RUFUS (King of England)

HENRY (King of England)

Plus loads of other children too

Short pants!

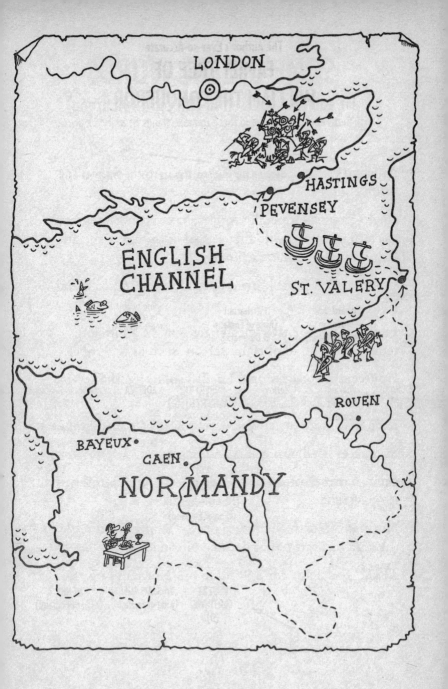

SOME USEFUL WORDS
(if you find yourself in 11th century Europe)

Atheling (as in 'Edgar the Atheling') Anglo-Saxon for 'prince'.

Anglo-Saxons Originally Angles, Saxons and Jutes from western Germany who first settled in Britain in the 5th century and became 'the English'!

Chain mail A flexible armour made from linked metal rings.

Emissary An agent or messenger sent on a mission, representing an important person (such as the pope).

Housecarl A professional English soldier in the service of the king.

Keep The large (usually square) tower of a medieval castle.

Magnates Medieval rulers and noblemen.

Mercenaries Professional soldiers who hire themselves out for payment.

Normans 'North Men'. Originally Vikings who settled in the area of France that became Normandy.

Thane The name for a 'lord' in pre-Norman England.

LITTLE WILLY – THE EARLY YEARS

William the Conqueror is most famous for winning the Battle of Hastings in 1066 and becoming the first real king of all England. The loser, King Harold, might have argued about the 'real king' part, but he was killed in the battle so had no say in the matter.

If there's one thing that had a huge effect on William's life it was luck – both good and bad – but when it really came to the crunch, it was nearly always good.

SON OF A TANNER'S DAUGHTER

Things didn't start off too well for young William. Back in the days when it could really matter if your mother and father were married or not, William's weren't and that earned him the nickname William the Bastard. His dad, Robert, was the younger brother of the Duke of Normandy, but his mum, wasn't Mrs Younger Brother of the Duke of Normandy. No, his mum was a tanner's daughter, and that made her a tanner too.

A tanner is someone who tans leather . . . and tanning leather involves giving leather that nice brown colour. A really popular way of doing this was to rub the leather with animal dung.

So William's dad was the all-important younger brother of the Duke of Normandy, but his mum was often up to her elbows in poo . . . something that didn't impress some of the other important folk in and around Normandy.

As well as William, Robert and Herleve (see – we're only on page 10, but already on first name terms) had another child: a girl they called Adelaide. But Robert was part of a noble family, and couldn't have a tanner's daughter as a girlfriend and certainly not as a wife.

A NEW MAN FOR WILLIAM'S MUM

Most historians agree that William's dad Robert was more than a little barmy – but he obviously cared for William's mother, so he found a rich man to look after her. (It was thought necessary for women to be 'looked after' way back then. Don't ask me why.) The man's name was Viscount Herluin of Conteville.

Herluin and Herleve had two children and the important one to remember was called Odo. You may think he's important because he became Chief of Security in the TV programme *Star Trek: Deep Space Nine™*, but that's a different Odo. This Odo grew up to be a brilliant warrior and a churchman, both at the same time! In fact, he became Bishop of Bayeux and if Bayeux sounds vaguely familiar, that's no surprise. The Bayeux Tapestry, made to commemorate William's great victory in 1066, is still in Bayeux to this day.

THE BAYEUX TAPESTRY

What we call the Bayeux Tapestry, the French call La Tapisserie de la Reine Matilde – in other words, 'Queen Matilda's Tapestry'. And who's Queen Matilda? William's wife, who became Queen of England soon after he became king. (You can find out more about her later.) For a long time, historians thought she designed and even made the Tapestry! We now know it was made on the instructions of William's half-brother Bishop Odo of Bayeux. What we call the Bayeux Tapestry isn't, in fact, a tapestry at all. Tapestries are woven on machines called looms. This so-called tapestry is really embroidery. It is about 230 feet (68 metres) long and every inch/centimetre was sewn by hand!

THE BIRTH OF WILLIAM

According to one medieval chronicler (also called William, but William of Malmesbury in his case) there was an 'omen' at William's birth, in 1027, that singled him out for great things. The trouble with many medieval chroniclers (people who kept written records of 'events') is that their so-called records of events were usually written a long time after these events were supposed to have happened . . . so we can't

be sure which facts are facts, which are half-truths and which are made up simply because they make good stories. According to this particular story, the moment William was born he clutched the reeds that covered the stone floor like a carpet and wouldn't let go. It took a number of midwives (the nurses there to help with the birth) to get the reeds from his tiny clenched fists. Here was a great warrior who would conquer and hold on to his conquests!

WILLIAM THE BASTARD

It's not very nice to call someone a 'bastard' nowadays, and it wasn't very nice back in William's day either. That, however, was the name William had to put up with before he became William the Conqueror.

In 1028, when his brother died, William's dad became Robert I, Duke of Normandy, better known as Robert the Magnificent. It can't have been much fun having a dad called Robert the Magnificent when you were called William the Bastard, but Robert had other names too. His enemies didn't think he was particularly magnificent. Some preferred to think of him as 'Robert le Diable', which may sound rather nice in French, but which actually means 'Robert the Devil'. He was said to be very cruel and nasty in battle.

TO THE HOLY LAND...

When William's father wasn't doing dreadful things, he was feeling guilty about the dreadful things he had done. He tried to put things right and get back into God's good books by building monasteries and, in the end, he decided that even that wasn't enough. To save his soul, he'd have to go on a pilgrimage to the Holy Land.

Robert paid for a huge number of other nobles, bishops and abbots to go with him. In fact, it's said that when his group of pilgrims passed through Constantinople – the city that's now called Istanbul – the locals thought he must be the king of all of France!

... WITHOUT WILLIAM

When Robert set off on the pilgrimage in 1034, William was only six years old so he left him behind. Before he left, Robert managed to convince the French magnates that, should anything happen to him and he fail to come back to Normandy, William was his heir and should become the next duke. The magnates agreed. This was an amazing feat because there was always a lot of infighting between the magnates, who were constantly jostling for power and control.

WILLIAM'S DAD DIES

It was lucky that Robert – who was supposed to be barmy, remember – made such careful plans in case he died, because the following year (1035) he did just that. He died of 'unknown causes' in a place called Anatolia and his body wasn't brought back to Normandy. The truth be told, no one even seems to know where he was buried, or what in . . . or if he actually was at all.

WILLIAM, DUKE OF NORMANDY

With his father dead, William was now Duke of Normandy at the age of seven. His great-uncle Robert was Archbishop of Rouen and gave William support. Support from the Church (with a capital 'C' and controlled by the Pope in Rome) was very important and added to the boy duke's strength.

Control of that part of Europe was based oaths of allegiance. 'Allegiance' is loyalty. If you swore allegiance to someone, you were supposed to be faithful to him . . . *supposed* to be. The barons of Normandy swore oaths of allegiance to their duke, the barons of Anjou and Flanders swore allegiance to their counts, and the duke and counts, in turn, swore allegiance to the King of France.

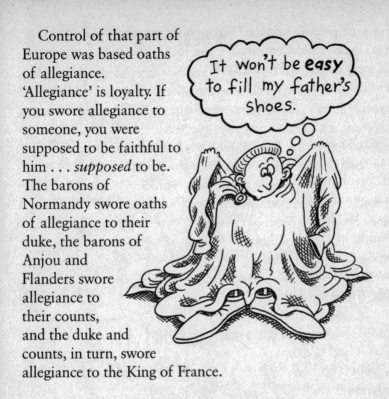

DEATH OF A GREAT-UNCLE

When William's great-uncle, the Archbishop, died in 1037, ten tough years followed. These were troubled times. Because he was a child, the young Duke William had grown-up guardians to look after him. Two (or three) of these were assassinated – which is just another way of saying murdered – and there were days when Normandy seemed pretty lawless. But it all turned out fine in the end. Thanks to support from King Henry I of France and the king's brother-in-law, Count Baldwin of Flanders, not only did Normandy come through the troubles unscathed, but William was still its duke.

SIR DUKE

In about 1041 or 1042, William was knighted by the king. This showed that each man respected the other and would protect him. According to yet another William, this was not greeted with great joy by everyone. William of Poitiers wrote that many French men and women were horrified at the thought of William the Bastard being a knight.

The problem was that not only would it make William even more powerful than he already was, but his family had originally been Viking raiders – huge bearded people attacking everything that moved, and frightening the life out of everyone. People feared that if you had a little Viking blood coursing through your veins, you couldn't help but cause trouble.

I didn't call you **Swill**. I simply said Arise Sir Will.

GOOD GUYS, BAD GUYS

William's first real military test came in 1047, when he was twenty years old. This was when Guy of Burgundy claimed that *he* should be the Duke of Normandy, not William! Guy was William's cousin. Guy's mother was William's Aunt Adeliza, sister of Robert the Magnificent. (Confusing isn't it?) Guy built support for his claim and the rebellion was carefully planned.

Fortunately for William, he still had King Henry of France on his side. A combined force of his and the king's men crushed the rebel army near Caen at a place called Val-ès-Dunes. This gave William a chance to show everyone what a good fighter he was . . . and he was good.

'MRS CONQUEROR' – MATILDA OF FLANDERS

In the days when a simple wrong word could lead to a punch-up or all-out war, it was important for William either to be friends with his neighbours, or to show himself to be more powerful than them. These were not the sort of neighbours who lived on the other side of the garden hedge; but were the rulers of the lands neighbouring Normandy: France, Anjou and Flanders.

One of these magnates was Count Baldwin of Flanders – the same Count Baldwin who'd helped protect William when his uncle had died – and he gave William permission to marry his daughter Matilda. (She was a descendant of the famous English king Alfred the Great.)

GOOD NEWS FOR SOME

This was good for Baldwin, because it meant that William, who was a respected fighter, would be on his side if he needed help. It was good for William because he could rely on Baldwin for help and, oh yes, he would get a wife out of it too. Some historical accounts suggest that William might even have *liked* Matilda, which was pretty unusual in marriages of these sorts.

Not so surprisingly, the King of France and the Count of Anjou weren't thrilled at the thought of Normandy and Flanders strengthening the ties between them. And they weren't the only ones. Someone called Leo IX was also far from happy with the arrangement. He made it crystal clear that there was no way that he would allow William and Matilda to marry.

S'not fair! I thought William was **MY** special friend!

PAPAL PROBLEMS

If Leo IX had simply been a king, or a duke or a count, William could have said 'I'll marry who I want to cos I'm bigger than you!' – he was five foot ten (1.78 metres), which was considered very tall way back then – and that might have been an end to it.

As it was, Leo was the Pope so he had a big say in such matters. The Church played a very important part in all the goings-on in Europe in those days, and the most important person in the Church was the Pope. Leo IX made his views very clear and very public at a meeting called the Council of Reims in 1049. Reims is a city in north-eastern France.

Today no one knows for sure why he was so against the marriage. Perhaps it was because William and Matilda were closely related. They were cousins. William's aunt was Matilda's granny.

But you've GOT to listen, I'm POPE!!!

WEDDED BLISS

When William and Matilda learnt what the head of the Church had to say, they waited a bit . . . then went ahead and married each other anyway. Like so many events in William's life (and in this period of history), we're not sure *exactly* when the ceremony took place – and don't believe anyone who confidently tells you otherwise – but it was probably round about 1053.

OFFICIAL BLESSING

By 1059, there was a new pope who accepted the marriage. Now, in the eyes of the Church, Matilda was the Duchess of Normandy. This wasn't simply out of the kindness of the new pope's heart. It was in return for William founding two new abbeys – St Stephen's and the Holy Trinity at Caen. This was the same Caen near which William had fought his first battle as duke.

The new pope was called Nicholas II, and it's only fair that his name should get a mention because Leo IX's has been six times so far.

THE ODD COUPLE

As those of you who have been paying attention will remember, William was tall for those days. Matilda was very small indeed. Next to William's five foot ten inches (1.78 metres), she was only four foot two (1.27 metres). We know Matilda's height not from another chronicler but from studying the bones found in her grave – which isn't the most cheerful way of measuring someone's height. (Matilda is often credited as being Britain's smallest monarch.)

KIDS GALORE!

William and Matilda were very happy together and had four sons – one called Richard died very young – and lots of daughters. No one seems to know for sure just how many daughters they had. It was probably five or six. The only one to be absolutely sure would have been Matilda, unless she lost count. This was at a time when sons were thought to be far more important than daughters because it was men (or boys) who inherited everything.

FAMILY IN HIGH PLACES

If marrying Matilda was good news for William, more came his way in 1060. Two of the French magnates died. Not only were the Count of Anjou and Henry I, the old king of France, now dead, but the new king, Philip I, was only a child.

Better still, who should be made 'regent' – ruling France on behalf of the king until he became a man? Why, Matilda's father, Count Baldwin of Flanders. That made him William's father-in-law! In Anjou, meanwhile, there was much squabbling between the nephews of the dead ruler over who should take his place.

With friends in the highest of places in France, and civil war in Anjou, William was now free to get invading without fear of interference.

OH, FOOLISH FOLK!

By now, William had a reputation as a solid and ruthless fighter, having used these skills against Brittany, Maine and Anjou and France. It was whilst attacking the walled French town of Alençon that the townsfolk taunted William. They hung tanned animal hides on the wall and made jokes about him being the bastard son of a tanner. This wasn't the brightest thing to do. He took thirty-four prisoners and had their hands and feet cut off and thrown over the wall into the town. The rest of the townfolk surrendered . . .

THE BUILD-UP TO BATTLE

Despite his reputation as a leader and a soldier, William didn't simply wake up one morning in 1066 and say, 'I've had a great idea, let's conquer England!' There were many events which led up to one of the most famous battles in history.

EDWARD AND THE VIKINGS

In Normandy, at about the time that William was knighted by the King of France (around 1041), lived an Anglo-Saxon who was to become Edward the Confessor, King of England. This man was to play a very important part in William's future. He was living in William's duchy (the proper term for a 'dukedom') rather than England because he was in exile. England was being ruled by Scandinavian Vikings, and they didn't want Edward around. He chose to come to Normandy because his mother was a lady known as Emma of Normandy (or plain 'Emma' to her friends).

ROYAL ENGLISH BLOOD

As well as being Edward's mum, Emma of Normandy was also William's great-aunt. Now, you couldn't exactly call a great-aunt the closest of relatives – William probably didn't bother sending her presents for Christmas and birthdays – but this relationship has a 'historical' importance. It meant that William was a blood relative of the English royal family, as well as being married to a descendant of King Alfred.

MARRIED TO TWO KINGS

Emma's first husband, and Edward's father, was the Anglo-Saxon king of England, Ethelred the Unready. Her second husband was the Scandinavian (Viking) king of England, king Cnut, sometimes called Canute. She and Cnut had a son, Edward's half-brother Harthacnut.

Cnut wasn't only king of England he was king of Denmark and king of Norway too . . . which sounds rather greedy, I'm sure you'll agree. It also shows how mixed up things were in those days.

EDWARD GETS THE JOB

When Harthacnut became king, he had no children so he decided that it was better that an Anglo-Saxon half-brother had the throne of England after him than some stranger. So, in 1041, Edward left Normandy to join Harthacnut who died soon after – very drunk – at the boozy wedding banquet of someone with the rather grand name of Tovi the Proud. He had only reigned for two years. Suddenly, Edward was king! The people were delighted. An Anglo-Saxon was back on the throne of England.

EDWARD AND HAROLD

A very important man in England at the time was Earl
Godwine and, in 1045, Edward married Godwine's daughter,
Edith. At the same time – not exactly the same time, of
course, I don't mean during the wedding ceremony – Edward
made two of Godwine's sons, Swein and Harold, into earls
too. (Godwine also had three other sons called Tostig, Gyrth
and Leofwine.) The important name to remember here,
though, is Harold: H-A-R-O-L-D, Earl of Wessex. He'll be
back. You can be sure of that.

A TURN FOR THE WORSE

Having spent so much time in exile in Normandy, it's not surprising to learn that Edward enjoyed spending time with Normans and French folk. As a result, he and the very English Earl Godwine had a few sticky moments, but things really began to turn bad when Edward appointed Robert of Jumieges as the new Archbishop of Canterbury (one of the most important positions in the English Church). As his name might suggest,

Robert of Jumieges was a Norman, and he most certainly wasn't Godwine's choice for the job.

GOODBYE, GODWINE!

In 1051, Edward's brother-in-law, Eustace of Boulogne, had a spot of bother with the people of Dover, a port on the Kent coast. Earl Godwine was supposed to discipline the townsfolk for their bad behaviour towards Eustace but he refused . . . so Eustace's forces assembled on one side and Godwine's supporters on the other.

This little local difficulty had turned into a threat to King Edward's authority. When the king lent support to Eustace, Godwine's supporters deserted the earl. They didn't want to challenge their king, so Godwine was ruined. He and many of his family fled abroad, including his daughter Edith (who was married to King Edward, remember) and son Harold (H-A-R-O-L-D). Some went to Flanders and others to Dublin in Ireland.

WILLIAM DROPS IN

A very useful source of information for historians studying this period is *The Anglo-Saxon Chronicle*. Although it sounds like a newspaper, it was actually a record of events that are supposed to have taken place at the time. The trouble is, there's more than one version of the chronicle (six, actually). Having just one version of events would have made life far too easy for historians!

According to one version, however, William, Duke of Normandy – yes, our William – came over to visit King Edward the Confessor in 1051. As a result, according to William of Poitiers (remember him?), the Archbishop of

Canterbury then went to Normandy to report that Edward had named William as his successor. In other words, when Edward died, William would become King of England!

TROUBLE AT HOME

There's no way of knowing whether this meeting really took place. The chronicler could simply have made it up to make William's claim to the throne seem more official later on . . . but King Henry of France *did* suddenly turn on William in 1052.

After years of treating William kindly, King Henry's forces invaded Normandy. The news that William had been promised the English throne (so was getting too big for his boots) was just the sort of reason why the King of France would have launched an attack. So maybe William really was named Edward the Confessor's successor. Or maybe he was simply spreading rumours that he had been named.

HERE'S HAROLD!

Meanwhile, back in England, Edward had his own problems. Godwine had turned up in Sussex, gathered support and marched to London. Like the time in Dover, there was no actual fighting, but this time it was the king who was forced to give way. He let Godwine back as an earl, Edith back as his queen and Harold (yes, H-A-R-O-L-D) as an earl too.

SPREADING CONTROL

Earl Harold grew more and more powerful in southern England. His brother Swein had died on his way back from a pilgrimage to Jerusalem, but another brother, Tostig, grew powerful in the North. By the early 1060s, Harold and Tostig were the most important earls in England (except for a region called Mercia) and had the Welsh under their thumbs. Scotland was ruled by Tostig's friend and ally Malcolm. With his daughter Edith as Queen of England, Earl Godwine's children now owned more land and riches than the king of England himself.

Some people reckon that the Godwines had more real power and influence than him too! (As Earl Godwine's son, Harold was sometimes referred to as Harold Godwineson.) Harold seemed the obvious choice to become king when the childless Edward the Confessor died . . .

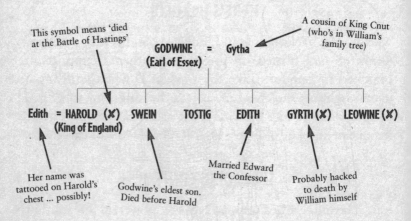

Just One Small Branch of
HAROLD'S FAMILY TREE
because most of his relatives have such silly names

This symbol means 'died at the Battle of Hastings'

A cousin of King Cnut (who's in William's family tree)

GODWINE (Earl of Essex) = Gytha

Edith = HAROLD (✗) (King of England)　SWEIN　TOSTIG　EDITH　GYRTH (✗)　LEOWINE (✗)

Her name was tattooed on Harold's chest ... possibly!

Godwine's eldest son. Died before Harold

Married Edward the Confessor

Probably hacked to death by William himself

WILLIAM MEETS HAROLD

According to the Norman version of events – in other words, this may never have happened – Harold and an armed escort set sail from Bosham in Sussex for either France or Normandy. Some say they were blown off course, others say they were shipwrecked, others suggested that they landed normally. Whatever the reason, Harold and his men found themselves in unfriendly territory and prisoners of Count Guy de Ponthieu. Because Harold was a nobleman, he was held to ransom. He would be treated well and would be released once a lot of money had been paid to Guy. As it turned out, Harold didn't have to wait that long. News of his capture had reached William.

Guy had sworn allegiance to the duke, so he had to release Harold to him on his orders. At last, one of the most powerful men in England was now face to face with the mighty 'Conqueror'. (Dramatic stuff, huh?)

FIRM FRIENDS

Again according to the Norman version, Harold and William became firm friends. Harold even accompanied William and his army against Duke Conan of Brittany. It was while crossing the river Couesnon on the way to war that Harold first showed William his bravery. Two Norman soldiers became stuck in quicksand at the water's edge and, risking his own life, Harold managed to save them. When the war against Brittany was over, William was the winner and 'gave arms to Harold', which was a bit like giving him a very important medal. This was an honour for Harold but, by accepting them, it also meant that he had to swear his loyalty to William.

SWEARING ON THE BONES OF SAINTS

By swearing allegiance to William, in William's castle in Bayeux – probably while he was touching caskets with sacred saints' bones inside – Harold was, in a way, accepting William as his boss and the rightful heir to the throne of England (if William wanted to be king). This was a BIG MOMENT in English history. Did Harold swear willingly? Was he forced? Did he ever really make such an oath at all? We'll probably never know for sure. But, according to the Normans, he then returned to England and to Edward the Confessor.

ANCIENT RELICS

Christian relics could be anything from saints' bones to pieces of the 'true cross' on which Christ was crucified. They were treated as sacred objects and some were thought to have incredible powers. Of course, many of these objects were not what they were supposed to be. There was money to be made in selling fake relics. If you put together all the so-called pieces of the true cross that were around at the time of William, you'd have probably been able to make a cross bigger than an aeroplane!

THE DEATH OF EDWARD

Edward the Confessor died on 5 January 1066. The next day, he was buried in Westminster Abbey, which had been built on his instructions in the 'Norman style'. In fact, it had only been finished and opened as a place of worship on 28 December just eight days before his death. With the king dead, there were three people quick to claim the right to the English throne: William, Harold and – to make things more confusing – someone else called Harald, but with an 'a'. Harald (with an 'a') was also known as Harald Hardrada which means 'Harald hard council' . . . and 'hard council' meant that you wouldn't want to mess with him in a hurry.

HARALD (WITH AN 'A')

Harald Hardrada was King Harald III of Norway and is considered by many people (who sit around and consider such things) as being the last of the Viking chieftains. Although he was 51 in 1066, he was still a great warrior . . . feared by many who didn't scare easily.

Harald Hardrada's claim to the English throne dated back to when Harthacnut was king of Denmark and king of England at the same time. It was agreed that, if Harthacnut died childless before Magnus King of Norway, Magnus should have his thrones. In the event Magnus only took on the throne of Denmark. When Harald became king after Magnus he staked the claim. In his mind England belonged to him.

Oh yes, I forgot to mention before that Harald Hardrada was almost seven feet tall (well over two metres) Yes. Almost seven feet. No wonder they called him 'the Norway Giant'!!!

KING HAROLD

On the very day that Edward the Confessor was buried, Harold, Earl of Wessex, had himself crowned king. *The Anglo-Saxon Chronicle* says that Harold was actually Edward's deathbed choice of successor, but he still needed to act swiftly now that the king was dead. Whether Edward did choose Harold or not doesn't change the fact that – according to the Norman version of events – Harold had sworn allegiance to William. That being the case, Harold should have asked William if he wanted to be king, or if he minded Harold becoming king instead. As it was, Harold simply claimed the throne of England for himself, without okaying it with anyone.

HALLEY'S COMET

According to the Bayeux Tapestry, a shooting star appeared as a bad omen at the time of Harold's coronation. Astronomers have now identified it as Halley's Comet which did genuinely appear in the sky in 1066, but not until the 24th April, long after the coronation and, anyway, in the past, the appearance of the comet had been seen as GOOD luck!

THE CONQUEST IS PLANNED

When news reached William in Normandy that Harold was now king, he must have been furious. There were a number of hastily arranged meetings between William and his barons at Caen, Lillebonne and at his palace at Bonneville-sur-Touques. The Norman barons were loyal to their duke and it was agreed that they should invade England and claim the crown of England for William because it was rightfully his. The Normans prepared for war.

WHIPPING UP SUPPORT

Before launching an attack across the English Channel, William wanted to make sure that he had as many rulers on his side as possible. There'd be no point in conquering England only to find that everyone else had turned against him. William was so powerful by then, that he had little trouble in convincing most of them. Even King Swein of Denmark had agreed not to get involved . . . and he was Harold's own cousin! But the most important person to have on his side was the Pope.

This pope was neither Pope Leo IX, who had forbidden William's marriage to Matilda, nor Pope Nicholas II, who had allowed it. This was a new pope called Alexander III.

HOLY RELICS!

William didn't go to see the Pope himself but sent his emissaries to argue his cause. They probably told Alexander III about Harold breaking the promise he'd made to William whilst touching the saints' bones. Popes used to get very touchy about people breaking promises they made

36

whilst touching saints' bones, so this would have been a good approach to take. Whatever was said to Pope Alexander, he agreed to support William's claim to the English throne. To show this support, he gave William's emissaries two important items: a banner that had been blessed by him, and a human hair. The banner was for William's troops to carry in battle to show that God was on the Normans' side. The hair was said to have come from the head of St Peter, Jesus's first disciple, so was the ultimate good-luck charm.

I said to bring me St. Peter's HAIR, fool: H-A-I-R !!

TIMBER!

If you'd been on holiday in Normandy in 1066, falling trees would have been a familiar sight. Throughout Duke William's duchy, trees were felled – chopped down, to you and me – and their trunks turned into the long planks used to build some of the ships that would be needed to cross the Channel for the conquest of England. These ships were built at Dives-sur-Mer (near Caen, again) on the Dives estuary and it was here that other ships were brought too. William's half-brother, Bishop Odo of Bayeux, provided 100 ships, whilst another half-brother, Robert, Count of Mortain, provided 120, and another 240 were provided by local magnates.

PEOPLE AND SUPPLIES

William wasn't only planning to take an army across the Channel with him, but their horses too. There would be about three thousand knights and esquires (trainee knights) on horseback and four thousand foot soldiers. That meant William needed a fleet that could carry about seven thousand people, three thousand horses and all their weapons and supplies too! All in all, about seven hundred ships had to be built . . . and the army had to be paid and fed before a single weapon was raised in anger.

THE NOT-SO NORMAN ARMY

Although William's attack on England was to become known as the Norman Conquest, a large number of those who fought alongside, in front of and behind him weren't Norman at all. As well as soldiers from Normandy, there were troops from Anjou, Brittany, Flanders, France and Maine. And they were all massed in and around Dives waiting to depart. It's an example of William's amazing leadership skills that they didn't strip the local countryside bare for everything they wanted. Forces such as these were used to taking what they wanted by force (hence the name). William, however, made sure that local peasants and farmers were left alone as much as possible.

ON THE MOVE

By 12 August, William's army was ready to set sail. Now all William needed to do was to wait for the right time to cross to England. Then, in late August or early September, he moved the whole fleet to St-Valéry-sur-Somme in Ponthieu. This had two great advantages over Dives-sur-Mer. Firstly, the crossing to England would be shorter from there. Secondly, it would take William's men straight into Harold's native Sussex.

THE WAITING GAME

Now William waited. For good weather? For good omens? For Harold to grow tired of waiting? We can't be sure, but we do know that William was, by now, a great soldier. He would have known that the longer he waited to attack, the more restless Harold would become in England and the more likely he would be to turn his attention to other troubles – because, boy, did King Harold of England have other troubles.

MEANWHILE, BACK IN ENGLAND

Things hadn't been easy for Harold ever since he took the crown. He had an uneasy alliance with two very powerful earls, a pair of brothers called Edwin and Morcar who were the earls of Mercia and Northumbria. He even married their sister, Edith, to try to keep in their good books, but the whole relationship was very shaky.

Then there was the problem he had with his brother Tostig, who he had ended up snubbing in favour of Edwin and Morcar. Harold had even played a part in exiling Tostig to Flanders not long before Edward the Confessor's death. In May, Tostig attacked southern and eastern England from the coast, a number of times. This meant that Harold had to use the army he'd prepared to fight William to force Tostig's men up north. This done, Harold's forces and fleet then waited for William's attack . . . and waited . . . and waited . . . The plan was to meet William's ships mid-Channel and fight them off before they even reached English soil. In the end, Harold sent his fleet back to London.

ATTACK ON YORK

In the middle of September 1066, King Harold was faced with a new problem. Tostig had joined forces with another claimant to the English crown: Harald (with an 'a') Hardrada. (You know, the frightening Viking chieftain who was almost seven feet tall.) Tostig and Harald's men arrived in a fleet of three hundred ships and terrorized the people along the coastline of Yorkshire. It's said that they even killed every single man, woman and child in the town of Scarborough.

While King Harold and his army hurried up north to face them, the city of York fell to the invaders. Being a Viking, it was usually Harald (with an 'a')'s policy to sack cities . . . in other words to reduce them to a pile of burning rubble. In this case, he agreed not to in return for hostages that he could ransom for lots of money.

THE BATTLE OF STAMFORD BRIDGE

There were to be 150 hostages, all of them children of important Yorkshire families, and Harald Hardrada was to

40

collect them at Stamford Bridge (which was about seven miles to the east of York). Harald and Tostig were still so pleased with themselves for having captured York that they became sloppy. They left a third of their army back with their ships, and the soldiers who had come with them weren't fully equipped. Many had even left behind their protective clothes – they never wore full armour anyway.

On the morning of 25 September, King Harold's army surprised and defeated them. This was the last important battle fought on English soil that didn't involve cavalry and archers. People fought hand-to-hand. It was a great victory for Harold and the English forces. The enemy may have arrived in 300 ships but so many were killed that only 25 ships were needed to carry them home.

King Harold felt on top of the world. Little did he know that Duke William of Normandy had, at last, set sail for England . . .

THE NORMAN CONQUEST

On 27 September, with a strong wind behind it, William's fleet set sail for England. It would have been an uneventful crossing if it hadn't been for two incidents. Firstly, the ship containing William's personal fortune-teller sank, drowning him. William was decidedly unimpressed. A fortune-teller who couldn't have predicted the sinking of his own ship wasn't of much use to him alive anyway! Secondly, the wind dropped, leaving William's command ship, the *Mora*, ahead of the others, unprotected and in sight of the Sussex coastline. Had Harold's fleet been ready and waiting, William might have been a 'sitting duck' and hacked to pieces before he'd even reached his destination. As luck would have it, though, Harold's men were hundreds of miles away in York. (Remember the part about William and luck?) The wind came up again, and William's armada reached the Pevensey – not Hastings – shoreline on 28 September.

FIRST BLOOD

Although there was no sign of a defending army, William was cautious and sent a party of foot soldiers to check out the area. All they found were frightened English peasants who'd heard horrible tales about what Normans did to their prisoners, and tried to put as much distance between themselves and these foreigners as possible.

Once William knew it was safe, he ordered his knights ashore. It was while climbing from the *Mora* that William himself fell flat on his face and gave himself a rather embarrassing nose bleed. This was one of those unlucky and awkward moments where William had to seize the moment to turn things to his advantage.

Snatching a fistful of dirt, he either said: 'See? I already have England in my grasp!' or 'By the glory of God, I have taken possession of my kingdom. The soil of England is in my hands!' or something in French that meant pretty much the same as either of these two quotes.

Whatever his exact words, William had his men cheering.

PEVENSEY CASTLE

William hadn't been the first to invade England along the Pevensey shore. The Romans had been there long before him and even built a fortress to guard it against future attack . . . but the Romans were long gone, and the fortress had fallen into ruin. In next to no time, William

43

had his men repairing the walls and his army set up camp there for their first night in England. The next day they moved on, but – after William became king of England – another of his half-brothers (Robert of Mortain) built a castle on the site.

Today, you can visit the ruins of the Norman castle in the middle of the ruins of the Roman fortress. Hidden amongst these ruins are World War II pillar boxes. These are gun emplacements set up to defend Britain against attacks from a 20th century German invasion force that never came.

DIGGING IN

The following morning, 29 September, William moved his army and fleet to Hastings where he built a wooden fortification in the town, probably on top of a mound built of sand and clay. Meanwhile, his army seized all the supplies they could from the surrounding land and terrorized the locals so that they wouldn't put up any resistance. The Bayeux Tapestry shows a mother and child fleeing from their house which has been set on fire by Norman soldiers.

HERE COMES HAROLD

News of William's landing can't have reached King Harold in York (enjoying his victory celebrations after the Battle of Stamford Bridge) until round about 1 October. By the 6 October, Harold and his army were back in London gathering reinforcements. By 13 October, they were already within striking distance of Hastings. There's no denying that he'd moved with incredible speed and efficiency.

44

Harold was a worthy opponent for William but he didn't have the Norman's luck.

THE BATTLE OF HASTINGS

One of the most common misconceptions – a big word for 'mistaken beliefs' – is that the Battle of Hastings took place at Hastings. You can see why people might think that. The clue is in the name: The Battle of *Hastings*. See? It does rather suggest that the battle took place at the place after which the battle was named – Hastings – doesn't it? Well, it didn't.

The name of the place where the Battle of Hastings took place is called Battle. You think I'm joking, don't you? Well, it's no joke. Of course, the place was called Battle *after* the battle, not before. That's how the town of Battle, about six miles north of Hastings, got its name in the first place. In fact, there wasn't even a town there at the time of the battle. There was a sort of hill which the Anglo-Saxons (Harold's men) called 'the place of the grey apple tree' and which the Normans called 'sandy lake' or 'senlac'. It was on top of Senlac Hill – more of a 'ridge' than a hill – that Harold and his army took up a defensive position.

GOD HELP US

As Harold's forces took up position along the ridge, with plans for seventy of his ships to guard the coast to ensure that William's men didn't try to escape by sea, William was busy offering prayers to God. He attended mass and even wore the saints' bones around his neck that Harold was supposed to have sworn on. (I expect he even spent a little time with St Peter's hair, so kindly given to him by the Pope, though no mention is made of this.) He then swore to God that if he won the battle on Senlac Hill, he would build an abbey on the site of his great victory.

Harold's problems were quite the opposite. As well as supporting William's cause, Pope Alexander III had also excommunicated Harold. In other words, he'd declared that the church would have nothing to do with him and that his prayers would be unanswered. Harold and his troops would be fighting a Godless fight.

THE OPPOSING ARMIES

Interestingly, Harold's and William's armies were probably about the same size as each other. Experts who are good at working out such things, reckon that there must have been about 7,000 men in each. The big difference was that William's army was made up of 3,000 knights and 4,000 infantry, archers and crossbow men, all of whom were hand-picked and highly trained.

Harold's army, on the other hand, was a mixture of trained soldiers, thanes, housecarls and even peasants armed with nothing more than rocks and sticks . . . and they all fought on foot. Anglo-Saxons thought fighting on horseback was for cowards only interested in a quick getaway!

OUTCLASSED

Harold's army was outclassed from the start. William's men, who were gathering to the south, at the foot of the slope where it wasn't so steep, hadn't fought a recent battle or been marching for days. His men were far better trained and far better equipped. If you get a chance to see the Bayeux Tapestry in Bayeux or the 19th century replica of the Tapestry in the Museum of Reading, in Berkshire, you can see all the different types of body armour the Norman invaders wore. Someone who took the trouble to count them all says there are seven kinds, including the cuir-bouilli – leather boiled in oil and moulded into the shape of the soldier's body. Once dried, it was incredibly tough and hard for a weapon to pierce.

WILLIAM'S ARMY DIVISIONS

Whereas Harold's army fought pretty much as one disorganized mass, with no soldiers in any particular roles, William's army was neatly divided into three divisions: the central division made up of Normans, directly commanded by William and Odo, the left division, made up mainly of men from Anjou, Brittany and Maine, under the command of Count Alan Fergant, and the right division, made up of men from Flanders and France, under the command of Count Eustace of Boulogne, and more Normans under the command of Robert of Beaumont.

At the front of each division were archers with short bows and crossbows. They didn't wear armour. Behind them were foot soldiers in chain mail, carrying swords and pikes. Behind them were the knights on horseback. The knights wore helmets and had chain mail down to their knees. (The horses themselves had no protection.) The knights had swords and spears, or lances and some carried maces.

HAROLD'S ARMY SHRINKS

Before battle commenced, some of Harold's soldiers went home. These men are described in various ways. Some suggest that they were simply deserters, terrified by the sight of William's organized army. Others suggest that these were men who had learnt of King Harold's excommunication by the Church and wanted nothing more to do with him. Florence of Worcester (a man, despite the name) says that they left because the battlefield was so narrow that they thought the army would be quite big enough without them. They'd only get in the way! The same is said in Robert Wace's *The Romance of Rollo*, a 12th century poem about the battle with a real anti-Harold flavour to it.

THE MINSTREL-KNIGHT

According to tradition, the first Norman to strike a blow at Harold's forces was Ivo Taillefer, William's minstrel-knight. He is supposed to have sung a song to his fellow knights, done some amazing tricks with his weapons in front of a gob-smacked enemy, then charged into their midst with sword flailing . . . only to be hacked to death in a matter of seconds.

THE BATTLE BEGINS

The Battle of Hastings began and ended in a single day, Saturday 14 October 1066. After speeches from both Harold and William to their men, they prepared to fight.

ADVANTAGE HAROLD

Although Harold's men had never had to fight knights on horseback in battle before, William's knights had never had to fight foot soldiers wielding battleaxes either. Harold's men inflicted terrible damage on the horses and the unprotected legs of their riders. It was the knights who came off worse, at first. They turned and fled, charging their horses through their own infantry and archers, down to the bottom of the valley.

Here the ground was marshy and there was a ditch that the knights promptly fell into. Some of Harold's army then charged down the hill after them and attacked the knights as they struggled to free themselves from their horses stuck in the mud.

WILLIAM DEAD?

About then, a rumour started to spread that William had already been killed in the fighting. As a result, the Norman division joined the retreat, followed swiftly by the French. William was, in fact, very much alive . . . and angry. He whipped off his helmet so that his men could see his face, threw himself in front of them, and, waving his sword, shouted: 'I am still living and, by God's help, shall yet have victory!'

As luck would have it – yes, luck played its part again – this was at about the time that a large flank of Harold's army had broken away from the others and were chasing after the despairing Normans. Now that they knew that their duke was alive and well, the Normans despaired no more and turned on their attackers. Cut off from the rest of the army, this large group of Anglo-Saxons were slaughtered by William and his men.

Delighted by this success, William's soldiers are then supposed to have carried out a 'tactical retreat', causing Harold's men at the other end of the field to charge after them. But this time it was a trick. The Normans suddenly turned on the Anglo-Saxons and killed them. This proved so successful, they did it a third time.

STANDING GROUND

Although Harold's army never launched a single concerted attack against the Normans, it never retreated either. This not only puzzled the Normans, but also historians to this day. One suggestion is that Harold felt doomed from the start and wanted to make this a final stand for himself and the proud families of England. Another is that there were simply too many soldiers to receive his orders.

William and his knights could charge about the battlefield on horseback shouting out instructions. Harold would have had to rely on foot messengers. The battlefield would have been too crowded to get orders to 7,000 men.

William was at the front of his men, on horseback, with the banner blessed by the Pope. Harold was behind his lines, on foot, unseen by those who were dying for him.

THE ARCHERS

Whether regrouping or sticking together for protection, the central core of Harold's army had gathered in one large cluster, holding up a protective wall of shields against the arrows of the enemy bowmen. An important moment in the battle came when William ordered his bowmen not to fire straight ahead at the enemy, but up in the air. This done, their arrows arched through the sky, sailing over the Anglo-Saxons' shields and raining down on their heads, killing or wounding them.

THE DEATH OF THE GODWINESONS

Harold's two remaining brothers, Gyrth and Leofwine Godwineson, fought with him in the battle. Both were killed. According to a version of events written by Guy of Amiens only two years or so after the battle (but not thought to be terribly reliable), Gyrth was killed by William himself. Gyrth's javelin killed William's horse so the duke launched himself at Gyrth 'like a snarling lion and hewed him limb from limb.'

Now in need of a horse, William ordered a knight from Maine to give him his, but the knight refused. Furious, William reached up, grabbed the knight by the nose-guard on his helmet and threw him head-over-heels off the back of the animal, then climbed into the saddle. When this horse, in turn, was killed, Eustace of Boulogne gave William his.

52

THE DEATH OF HAROLD

One of the great debates about the Battle of Hastings is just how King Harold died, once the Normans broke through the enemy lines. Many have believed for a long time that Harold was killed with an arrow through the eye. This is based on a scene shown in the Bayeux Tapestry. None of the early written accounts of the battle mention the arrow at all. The earliest mention was written in 1099, and could have been written after seeing the Tapestry. It is fashionable to argue nowadays that the man in the Tapestry pulling the arrow from his eye isn't meant to be Harold at all – that honour goes to another man who has been 'run through' by a sword. There are even those who suggest that Harold is both men . . . struck by an arrow then run through when blinded. We don't know and, unless someone invents a time machine and goes back and checks, we will never know for sure. What we *do* know is that Harold died.

I do wish you'd stop saying 'Eye, eye, Sir!'

LAST DITCH ACT

Clearly defeated, some of Harold's few remaining Anglo-Saxon troops carried out one final act against the victorious Norman army. As dusk fell and the surviving losers went to hide out in the countryside, a group of them deliberately led a significant number of William's knights into a hidden ditch, killing many of them.

BATTLE ABBEY

The chroniclers make it clear that the dead Harold could not be identified by his face but by certain marks on his body. There are those who claim that these marks were a tattoo which read: 'Edith and England'. This Edith wasn't his sister (wife of Edward the Confessor), but his own wife Edith.

As he had promised to God, William had an abbey built on the site of the battlefield. Its high altar was built on the spot where Harold's body was found. Though that part of the abbey no longer stands, the spot is still marked with an inscribed stone slab. (I know. I've been there to check.)

WHAT NEXT?

With Harold dead, William had rather hoped that the English magnates (what was left of them) would immediately offer him the crown. They didn't. In fact, Edgar the Atheling (a great-grandson of Ethelred the Unready) was declared king by his supporters in London. After butchering the citizens of Romney – who'd killed a party of foraging Normans – and securing the port of Dover and taking Canterbury, William and his troops then marched on Southwark, where houses were burnt and English soldiers retreated across London Bridge. William then crossed the Thames at Wallingford sending many raiding parties to cause mischief and mayhem as well as to gain supplies. He had successfully entered London.

WILLIAM – THE REMAINING YEARS

William was crowned King of England on Christmas Day 1066 in Westminster Abbey by the Archbishop of York. This moment marked the official end of the invasion. Now the only people who'd find themselves in trouble from William's soldiers were English rebels who didn't accept him as king. Everyone else would be treated as subjects under his protection. Well, that was the idea, anyway. When crowds outside the abbey cheered and shouted for their new king, Norman soldiers thought they had a riot on their hands so set fire to nearby houses for good measure!

ON STANDBY FOR WAR

Although William had won the Battle of Hastings and taken control of London, he knew that, to stay one step ahead of the enemy, he needed to keep much of his army on a 'war footing' – ready to fight rebels at a moment's notice. He immediately had a wooden castle built in London which, in 1078, was replaced with a stone keep he had built by Gundulf (later Bishop of Rochester).

This massive building was to remind the English just how mighty and powerful their Norman masters were. Rumours spread that the red mortar used to hold the stones in place was made from the blood of William's enemies. (It was really made from ground-up Roman red-bricks.) Once finished and whitewashed, the keep became known as the White Tower. This later became the central building in what is now the Tower of London.

THE LAWS OF THE LAND

William didn't change everything on becoming king. He had claimed that he was Edward the Confessor's chosen successor, so he kept many of Edward's laws and kept many Anglo-Saxon institutions and their way of working. He gave his Norman followers land and titles and many of these new barons started off by treating the native English badly, resulting in a series of revolts.

HOMEWARD BOUND

Although there were still pockets of rebel resistance throughout England, William felt confident enough to nip back home to Normandy in March 1067. There were probably two reasons for this confidence. Firstly, he left his half-brother Odo in charge of Dover and the Kentish ports (so messages could easily be sent across the Channel). Secondly, he took a whole host of important English hostages with him. They set off from Pevensey – the very place where William's invasion had landed (and he'd had the embarrassing nosebleed). Back home, he held parties in Rouen and Fécamp to celebrate his victory. William returned to England in December.

THE FAMILY

Matilda came over to England 'with a great attendance of knights and noble women' in 1068. She was officially crowned Queen at Winchester. She later gave birth to their fourth son, Henry. Their oldest boy Robert was to become the next Duke of Normandy, their second son William Rufus was William's successor to the throne of England and this little Henry was to follow his brother to the throne as Henry I. Their daughter Adela was to become the mother of Stephen, Henry's successor. Robert's nickname was 'Curthose' – which meant 'shortpants' – because he had stubby legs. At least it was better than being called 'the Bastard', like his dad.

Get this thing off me!

UPS AND DOWNS

In the same year, Harold's mother led an uprising in Exeter. In the year 1069 alone, William was faced with attempted uprisings in Chester, Dorset, Durham and York as well as an invasion from King Swein of Denmark who actually managed to take control of York, and parts of Lincoln before being forced out! It wasn't until 1070 that the last of the major uprisings were finally quashed – a good word that – and that all the English nobles who had survived the Battle of Hastings were now dead. Two later rebellions (in East Anglia in 1075 and Northumbria in 1080, following the murder of the Bishop of Durham), and the threat of further invasion from the Danes made life difficult for William throughout his reign.

TROUBLE AT HOME

At the same time as being the new King of England, William was still the old Duke of Normandy and had troubles at home too. In 1078, his own son Robert ('shortpants') even led a revolt in Normandy! William and Robert came to an uneasy agreement (with Matilda sticking up for their boy). Then, in 1082, William had trouble with another family member. This time it was Odo. Apart from stating that he was disloyal, history doesn't record Odo's actual crime against his half-brother. But whatever it was, it was enough for William to have him arrested on the Isle of Wight and imprisoned at Rouen, where he remained until William's death.

THE DEATH OF MATILDA

Queen Matilda died in 1083 and, according to William of Malmesbury, William wept for many days. The woman he loved had died. Following her wishes, William – by now very fat as well as tall – had his tiny wife's body buried in the church of the Holy Trinity at Caen.

THE DOMESDAY BOOK

In 1086, William ordered the putting together of one of the most important historical documents of all time. Of course, he didn't know that was what he was doing, but it was still obviously an amazing undertaking even then. This was to be the Domesday Book, a list of who owned what land and property throughout England . . . so that William would know who owed him what by way of 'dues'. William needed to raise money to pay his mercenaries. He needed these because his son Robert appeared to be about to form an alliance with King Philip of France against him and, although locked away, the odious Odo still seemed to have some influence with William's enemies. William was to die before the book was completed.

What the Domesday Book gives us today is an almost complete picture of the make-up of England at the time – from the settlements wasted by the crushing of rebellions, to the ownership and location of houses still standing to this day.

ENOUGH IS ENOUGH

In 1087, Philip of France's forces seized territory inside Normandy. William was in England at the time, but soon gathered together his own forces and crossed the Channel to France. William wanted to teach Philip a lesson, so destroyed the French towns of Chaumont, Pontoise and Mantes – looting, pillaging and burning. It was at Mantes that William was himself injured (or, possibly, taken ill). He was in a terrible state and was taken to Rouen.

THE DEATH OF WILLIAM

Rouen was too noisy a place for William. He was dying. They moved him west to a house in the priory of Saint-Gervais. Two of his sons, William and Henry, were at his bedside whilst the third, the snake-in-the-grass Robert, was off sucking up to the French king. Despite this, William named Robert as his successor to the duchy of Normandy. He chose, however, to give the English crown to William . . . which really annoyed Robert when he found out! William gave Henry £5,000 in silver but predicted great things for the boy. Then, early on the morning of 9 September, moments after the bell for prayer rang out from Rouen Cathedral, he died.

THE HOUSE STRIPPED BARE

With the duke and king now dead, all the magnates who had been attending him hurried away to make sure that they were at home to defend their property. Who knew what problems there might be, now that there was a sudden shift in power? With their master gone, William's attendants decided that this would be an excellent opportunity to steal everything in sight. They took everything from the smallest plate, to robes, linen and the biggest pieces of furniture. When they'd finished, they left William's half-naked body lying in the middle of the floor in an empty room.

THE FUNERAL

If you think that's undignified, wait until you hear what happened at the funeral. Before William's body even reached the church of St Stephen in Caen, fire broke out on the route of the funeral procession. The crowds that had gathered to pay their respects now dashed off to try to put out the flames instead . . . so the monks had to carry out the funeral service on their own.

Once inside the church, they found that William's rather large body was too big to fit inside his stone coffin. The stonemason hadn't bothered to take measurements. There was no option but to make William fit, so the monks had to try to stuff him in the coffin with some force. As a result, William's bowels burst, filling the church with a stench so horrible that even clouds of incense couldn't disguise it . . . The priests rushed through the service and left as quickly as possible.

Run for your lives! He could **explode** any minute!

AND THERE'S MORE . . .

If you thought nothing more unfortunate could happen to William's remains, you'd be wrong. In 1562, William's tomb was opened up during a disturbance and his bones scattered everywhere. All that was retrieved was a single thighbone which was promptly given a Christian reburial . . . but even that one remaining bone wasn't left in peace. During the French Revolution, William's tomb was demolished. Why? Because, even 700 years after his death, William the Conqueror, Duke of Normandy and King of England, was seen as a symbol of great wealth and power.

TIMELINE
At home and abroad

1027   'William the Bastard' is born to Robert and
        Herleve.
        *The first fireplaces with mantelpieces are under
        development in Western Europe!*

1028   William's barmy dad, Robert, becomes Duke of
        Normandy.

1035   The devilish Robert the Magnificent dies, so
        William becomes the duke.

1040   *Macbeth kills Duncan and becomes King of the
        Scots.*
        Movable type is used for printing in China.

1041   Edward the Confessor becomes King of
        England.

1045   *First formula for gunpowder is published in
        China.*

1047   William defeats cousin Guy of Burgundy at
        Val-ès-Dunes.

1053(ish) William marries Matilda.

1055   *Turks take control of Baghdad*

1058   *Arab conquest of West Africa begins*

1065   Westminster Abbey is completed

1066   5 January: Edward the Confessor dies.
        6 January: Edward buried and Harold declares
        himself King of England.
        25 September: Harold defeats Harald (with an
        'a') and Tostig at Battle of Stamford Bridge

1066	27 September: William sets sail for England
	28 September: William lands at Pevensey. (Ooops! That nosebleed!)
	14 October: William defeats Harold at Battle of Hastings
	25 December: crowned King of England.
1067	First stitches of Bayeux tapestry are sewn.
1086	Domesday Book begun.
1087	William dies in Normandy. His second (living) son, William Rufus becomes William II.
1090(ish)	*Persian poet Omar Khayyam writes* The Rubaiyat. *Still in print today.*
1094	*Spanish hero El Cid takes Valencia.*
1100	William II dies. His brother Henry becomes King of England.